LIFE IS LIKE
A RUBIK'S CUBE

DERRICK STANDIFER

This Is The Year For
Your New Book

W W W . S E L F P U B L I S H N 3 0 D A Y S . C O M

Published by Self Publish -N- 30 Days

Copyright 2020 Derrick Standifer

Printed in the United States of America

ISBN: 979-8-60347-005-4

1. Motivational 2. Self Help 3. Problem Solving 4. Success

Derrick Standifer Life is Like a Rubik's Cube

Disclaimer/Warning:
This book is intended for lecture and informative purposes only. This publication is designed to provide competent and reliable information regarding the subject matter covered. The author or publisher are not engaged in rendering legal or professional advice. Laws vary from state to state and if legal, financial, or other expert assistance is needed, the services of a professional should be sought. The author and publisher disclaim any liability that is incurred from the use or application of the contents of this book.

I am a community child, meaning I was raised by a lot of amazing people who have invested in me. If I started naming individuals, I would surely leave someone off. You are all greatly appreciated more than you know. This dedication is to the community of people who raised me. To my parents who passed away from cancer, I know that you are looking down on me. To my babies, Ayana and Derrick Jr., I know that you are looking up to me.

TABLE OF CONTENTS

Introduction. 1

STEP ONE
Belief 7

STEP TWO
Solve Your Cross. 29

STEP THREE
Fill in Your Corners. 39

STEP FOUR
Take It to the Next Level 59

STEP FIVE
See the Bigger Pictures. 69

STEP SIX
Do NOT Take the Stickers off . . 79

Conclusion. 89

"People are always blaming their circumstances for what they are. I don't believe in circumstances. The people who get on in this world are the people who get up and look for the circumstances they want, and if they can't find them, they make them."
— **GEORGE BERNARD SHAW**

"The greater the obstacle, the more glory in overcoming it."
— **MOLIÈRE**

"I am more than my scars."
— **ANDREW DAVIDSON**

"You gain strength, courage and confidence by every experience in which you really stop to look fear in the face. You are able to say to yourself, 'I have lived through this horror. I can take the next thing that comes along.' You must do the thing you think you cannot do."
— **ELEANOR ROOSEVELT**

WHENEVER I HEAR PEOPLE TALK about the trials and tribulations of life, I always advise to overcome the trial, put it in a book, and tell the world how they did it so that others can be encouraged by their story. This book is me taking my own advice and telling my story of how I used the Rubik's Cube to navigate the twists and turns of life.

Tragedies can paralyze us if we let them. Sometimes, we may feel that God is bullying us because of the tragedies that we have to endure. Personally, I felt that God was mad at me, but then I realized that God was using me. God had placed a series of tests in my life for me to turn into a *test*imony. Often, I thought that my load was too heavy to carry. Many times, I wanted to give up on life altogether. Then, I heard a line in a speech that gave me new life. "God gives the heaviest burdens to the strongest people." So, I saw my burdens as a test of strength, not an attempt to break me.

Ironically, my life took a rough turn left soon after I graduated from Carver Early College High School. What made it ironic was that I was voted by the student body as 'Most Likely to Succeed,' Homecoming King and Student Government Association President. I was also a National

Coca Cola Scholar and the Salutatorian of my graduating class. With all these accolades, one would assume that my post-high school career would be an immediate path to success; unfortunately, that was furthest from the truth.

Since I graduated Salutatorian, Howard University offered me a full tuition scholarship to their institution. However, I foolishly took a different and unlikely path, a path that led me to Florida Agricultural and Mechanical University in Tallahassee, Florida. I received a partial scholarship to attend this school, and the majority of my education was to be paid for by student loans. Knowing that I was taking out student loans to pay for school when I was offered a full-tuition scholarship to Howard, made me feel like a complete idiot.

Like most college students, I coped with my problems by indulging in vices that were not conducive to my growth, like drinking and smoking weed. My grades significantly dropped. By my second year at FAMU, I ended up losing my partial scholarship. I felt like a failure because of the student loans that I was accumulating and for doing so poorly in school. I got so down on myself that I dropped out of FAMU and came back home to attend Georgia State University.

Thinking that I would be able to excel at Georgia State, I was still distracted by everything that caught my attention and did everything except my school work. I was hosting poetry shows and skipping class to smoke weed. This was mixed with this notion that I would become a world-renowned poet. Basically, I had no use for school. I was so academically poor at GSU that I earned a 0.0 GPA during my matriculations. That is not a typo; my GPA during the one year that I was student at GSU was literally a 0.0. I basically stopped going to class and did not make school a priority.

During that time, I started waiting tables. It was good money, but dropping out of school to wait tables is not exactly the wisest career choice long-term. Kanye West had a song on his critically acclaimed album, "College Dropout," called School Spirit. In the song, Kanye West said, "This brother graduated at the top of our class, I went to Cheesecake, and he was a waiter there." I looked at myself and here I am, a dropout at one school and a flunk out at another, and for work I am a professional waiter and part-time poet.

This truly was one of the lowest moments in my life. There were students whom I had mentored that were graduating college before I had done so. I remember going back to my school to volunteer and one of my mentors, Dr. Thomas Gosha, asked me, "Are you not embarrassed?"

"This brother graduated at the top of our class I went to Cheesecake, he was a waiter there." — KANYE WEST

I couldn't even respond. I felt like a failure. I let a lot of people down who invested in me. I was consumed by suicidal thoughts, but I was desperate not to stay there. I remember listening to a speech by Les Brown. His words stuck with me as if they were glued to my forehead. He said, "Just because you fail, it does not mean you are a failure." You can always bounce back from your trials and tribulations.

I decided to do something about my situation. Instead of being down and depressed, I chose to be a victor, not a victim. I had to accept that I am responsible for my life. I am the one who determines how my sail will flow. This was a profound change in my mindset.

"I am responsible for my life."

Prior to re-enrolling in school, I blamed my high school counselor for encouraging me to attend FAMU. I wrote letters to people about how she was to blame for my situation. I did whatever I could to take the blame off of me and put onto someone else. However, my life transformed when I made the decision to be the "Master of my Faith and the Captain of my Soul," (from a poem by William Ernest Henley). It was then that I took full responsibility for my decisions. It changed my life for the better.

I decided to go back to Tallahassee and finish what I had started. I went back to FAMU reborn. The old, lazy Derrick had died, and a new me stepped foot on the "highest of seven hills." I went on to earn a bachelor's degree, and a year later I was fortunate and highly favored to earn my master's degree. I accomplished it all while battling homelessness and the unexpected birth of my daughter, Ayana.

Afterwards, I embarked on the journey of educating students to step into their greatness and excel academically. This experience was memorable in that I was able to live my passion of teaching children, but it was traumatizing and almost broke me. During my first year of teaching, I experienced the trauma of losing my mother to cancer one week before my 26th birthday. My only uncle died from cancer three months later. My wife and I had given birth to our son, Derrick Jr. during this time. This was a rocky time for our marriage. We did not survive it and got a divorce. All of this happened so fast and suddenly. I was sad and depressed all the time. I smiled in everyone's face; nobody knew that my world was crumbling around me. However, it was the steps that I have outlined in this book that kept me from breaking from the weight that life had placed upon my shoulders.

This is me, putting my journey into a book, not for your enjoyment, but most importantly, as an instrument for your empowerment. I hope that you are encouraged to not make excuses and to prevail when life has given you more than you *think* you can take. In this book, the Rubik's Cube serves as a metaphor for a prime goal that you would like to accomplish in life. It is important to remember that every individual's Rubik's Cube is different. Some may want to become a world-class athlete, others may desire to become a politician. Whatever it is that you desire, the steps to accomplishing your goals and the steps to solving the Rubik's Cube are similar.

There are six Steps, each explaining how to metaphorically solve a different step in solving the Rubik's Cube inside of you.

- Step One *is to believe that you can solve your Rubik's Cube.*

- Step Two *is solving your cross or finding a strong "Why!"*

- Step Three *is filling in the blanks, which is a metaphor for surrounding yourself with positive people, and in-taking positive motivational messages on a consistent basis. You'd be amazed at the wonders that it will work in your life.*

- Step Four *is taking it to the next level, which means to continue to grow and get better.*

- Step Five *is seeing the bigger picture and enduring the storms of life.*

- Step Six *is don't take off the stickers. This book will be filled with twists and turns, but we will ultimately reach a point where you learn how to solve the Rubik's Cube inside of you.*

Just because you fail, it does not mean that you are a failure.

— UNKNOWN

STEP ONE
BELIEF

PART ONE

THE FIRST STEP TO SOLVING the Rubik's Cube is to simply believe that you can solve it. Have you ever picked up a Rubik's Cube, turned it a few times, thought that you discovered the formula, and finally realized that solving the Rubik's Cube was harder than you imagined? Did you give up and throw it down in frustration? No need to be embarrassed, you are not alone. This was my first experience with the Rubik's Cube as well. I told myself that only geniuses knew how to solve it, which is true, but what is also true is that everyone has a genius inside of them. However, our public school system has been judging too many people by a slew of learning elements, which do not always demonstrate an individual's genius level. Albert Einstein said, "Everybody is a genius, but if you judge a fish by its ability to climb a tree, it will live its whole life believing that it is stupid."

Before you can solve the Rubik's Cube or anything in life, you must first believe that you can solve it. It is essential for you to have confidence and faith that you can make it happen. Nobody has ever solved the Rubik's Cube without first believing that they can solve it.

When I witness people's interaction with the Rubik's Cube, it is quite similar to people's interaction with life. Oftentimes, we will pick up the Rubik's Cube and *try it*, but once it gets too hard, we give up and move on to something easier. Almost instinctively, people see the Rubik's Cube and proclaim how they cannot solve it because they are not smart enough. Instead, they should declare that they believe that they can solve it.

"You have to expect things of yourself before you can do them."
— MICHAEL JORDAN

The Rubik's Cube is the perfect instrument to exhibit the power of belief to doubters. At first, when you pick up the Rubik's Cube, it seems difficult. With no plan of action, the Rubik's Cube can almost seem impossible, like an endless sequence of twists and turns. And if it becomes too frustrating, doubters throw in the towel and develop a false belief that solving the Rubik's Cube is impossible. However, those who pick up the Cube and develop the confidence that they *will* solve it, take the necessary steps to do so.

Those who don't want to take the necessary steps will either make excuses or look for something easier. Easier doesn't always mean better. I remember being in an Economics class and one of the students had performed poorly on a test. Her response was, "I'm transferring to Education, this is too hard!" The first problem is that she did not have the confidence in herself to elevate; the second problem is, sadly, she will project her lack of self-confidence on to her students. Hence, why it is vital that we are conscious of the people in our inner circle. (A concept that I will revisit in Step Three: Fill in Your Corners.)

Obtaining the confidence and belief in one's ability to do anything is critical. Belief is usually the deciding factor in whether or not someone can accomplish what they set out to do. Mr. Horace Dukes, founder and CEO of the Dukes Foundation, a mentoring organization **SOMETIMES WE HAVE TO BORROW BELIEF IN OURSELVES FROM OTHER PEOPLE IN ORDER TO SEE IT WITHIN OURSELVES.** in Atlanta, once said, "I can take a student with the highest intellectual capabilities, the best athletic abilities, but if he/she does not have confidence, then I will show you a failure every time. However, if I take a student with none of those strengths, but he/she has confidence that he/she can be successful, then I will show you a success most of the time." Confidence offers one an advantage over those who don't possess confidence. The main difference between those who know how to solve the Rubik's Cube and those who don't is their belief of whether or not they can solve it.

According to the Merriam Webster dictionary, the definition of belief is "a state or habit of mind in which trust or confidence is placed in some person or thing." Belief is not a minute phenomenon. The concept of belief was strong enough to build the United States of America into arguably one of the most powerful countries in human history from a group of colonists who sought freedom. Belief was the tool that allowed Haiti to defeat the powerful French army to become the first black independent nation in the free world.

Belief is a builder of nations; it is a writer of best-selling novels; it is the catalyst of all things purposeful, and the world suffers when people have a lack of belief in themselves and their God-given skillsets.

Belief allows us to judge an idea or principle by our perspective of what we deem to be true. When we first believe that we can solve the Rubik's Cube, the hardest part is conquered. It takes absolute faith and confidence to accomplish goals and overcome the obstacles that come along with them. In most cases, we possess a burning desire when we genuinely believe in something. When people wholeheartedly believe in something, they envision it in their mind's eye. They know what they want specifically, and the picture in their mind is as vivid as if it were directly in front of them.

Science does not typically prove that belief is valid enough to obtain success. As in the case of Roger Bannister, who was the first person to run a mile in under four minutes, many people thought that the feat was merely impossible. There were rumors that the human lungs would explode if a person did run the mile in under four minutes. Bannister accepted the venture with the belief that it could be done. Since then, thousands of distance runners have accomplished the feat because they saw the accomplishment being realized.

Before a farmer sows a seed into the ground, they must first see the return of their labor. If one plants oranges, they must understand what the production of oranges looks like before a harvest. The vision has to be so succinct that they can describe the type of oranges, give an estimate of how many oranges the tree produces, and how frequently the orange tree will bear new fruit.

The farmer bets his livelihood, and that of his family's, that the seeds will meet the expectation of producing fruit. The farmer willingly invests time, energy, and resources into the production of these oranges. He knows the steps from the start until the finished product, and his confidence ultimately yields the results. The time, energy and resources are equally important as the belief. However, it is belief that propels us in motion.

> ## "Faith is taking the first step even when you don't see the whole staircase."
> ## — MARTIN LUTHER KING, JR.

Having the Rubik's Cube in my hand for the first time was so frustrating, especially since I did not have a guide on how to solve it. Belief was the agent that told me I could get it done. I had seen it completed before, and I was determined to get it solved by any means necessary. I could see the production of my belief in crystal clear form. After failing a countless number of times, I finally met my goal of solving the Rubik's Cube. Again, it was my belief, faith, and confidence that catapulted such an endeavor.

WHY BELIEVE IN YOURSELF?

The most pertinent reason to believe in yourself is because beliefs determine the future. Confucius once popularly affirmed, "He who says he can and he who says he can't are both usually right." As you start to believe in yourself, your confidence begins to rise. Your performance simultaneously increases once your self-esteem does.

There are numerous studies that conclude that self-confidence is a vital ingredient of success. People operate and interact with others based on the belief in their abilities that they have. Wherever confidence resides, success is most likely to live as well; an absence of progress is due to deficient belief in self. In other words, self-confidence provides one with an "aha!" moment of "I can do this." We trust our bodies to achieve what we know it can, but our confidence or lack thereof tells us precisely what our bodies can and cannot take.

Without self-confidence, we wouldn't know what we are even capable of executing. We have to test our limits to know what we can do. After we know what we can do, we are then capable of elevating ourselves. Confidence provides us with the assurance that we can elevate.

EVELYN WAUGH, "IF WE ARGUE FOR OUR LIMITATIONS, THEN WE GET TO KEEP THEM."

As a teacher, I see my students live out this phenomenon every day. The students who excel academically, and in other areas of their lives, are those who believe that they can do so. Other students may need an extra push and some encouragement. Sometimes students do not know what believing in themselves looks like, and that is when it is our opportunity to push our belief onto our students. Sometimes this borrowed belief can be the advocator in activating the greatness that exists in each of our young people.

BORROWING BELIEF

I've always had crooked teeth. What's crazy is that I've had braces before, and I still have crooked teeth, but that's another story. My subpar smile caused me to have low confidence in many areas of my life. I did not believe that I was well-liked or even well-respected during high school.

One day my counselor asked me why wasn't I running for any positions in the student government association. I told her that not enough people would vote for me to win. She believed in me and saw something in me that I did not see in myself.

As a result of her confidence in me, it encouraged me to have faith in myself. Sometimes we have to borrow belief in ourselves from other people in order to see it within ourselves. I was even too scared to submit my name for participation. I barely had friends in high school, let alone enough people to vote for me. The other people who were running were friends of mine, and I just knew that one of them would win.

I knew that I had to exercise creativity and uniqueness to claim the victory, so I wrote a poem, which was a great alternative to their traditional speeches. The next day all of the votes were counted, and they not only stated that I was named Homecoming King, but also won the vote for SGA president! I was shocked and did not believe it.

Some students were so mad that they made a petition to verify the votes. I went to the SGA advisor and told him that if I had unrightfully won the elections, I didn't want it. He said, "You think that low of yourself, that you can't even believe that you won?"

That is when I realized the value of having people in our corners who love and support us even when we don't believe in doing so for ourselves. I would have never run for those positions if I had not been encouraged by others.

I did not know that so many people respected me enough to represent the school in that capacity, and still to this day I wonder how I was able to do so. I did not have the confidence to see myself as a school leader. However, I learned the significance of a valuable inner circle with mentors who will motivate you to challenge yourself.

"When we expect certain behaviors of others, we are likely to act in ways that make the expected behavior more likely to occur." — UNKNOWN

Building confidence in others is the main reason why I want to teach as many people as possible how to solve the Rubik's Cube. I knew that the Rubik's Cube would change people's outlook on themselves, and it would also change others' perspective of them.

In a report published in 2015, entitled "Educational Challenges of the Rubik's Cube!" Sander Kiss writes that, "the Rubik's Cube builds confidence." So many people associate the Rubik's Cube with having a supreme genius talent, yet the Rubik's Cube is very simple to solve if you are willing to commit to a few short series of lessons.

One of my students was teaching another student how to solve the Rubik's Cube, and he constantly used the word "algorithm." After praising him for teaching, I told him that he had to stop using the word "algorithm" when teaching new people. The word "algorithm" may be frightening for beginners and can be a deterrent. Instead, use the colors to tell how to solve the cube. We have to show people how simple solving life, as well as the Rubik's Cube, can be. Life can either be these sets of algorithms or matching colors with colors.

Unfortunately, there are souls on the planet who do not believe in themselves, and there are those who make it their mission to find every reason why they should doubt themselves. They question their ability to succeed. These are the people who are not aware of the words of Evelyn Waugh, "If we argue for our limitations, then we get to keep them." It is unbelievable that a large number of people have mastered the saying

"What if?" Every time you give them a solution to one of their myriad of problems, they tend to respond with, "Well, what if _____ doesn't happen?" This statement refers to the negative aspects of the situation and pays minimal energy to the world of positive possibilities.

> ## "Low self-esteem is like driving through life with your handbrake on."
> ## — MAXWELL MALTZ

We all know that one person who has the talent and prowess to be a world-class athlete, author, or entrepreneur, but they don't believe in themselves. We can point out time and time again examples of their genius, but they always doubt it. Maybe they don't think they could be great because they believe certain people are born great.

Malcolm Gladwell's concept of "The 10,000 Hour Rule" states that it takes an individual 10,000 hours to truly master one goal. The Chinese proverb reads, "The difference between the master and the beginner is that the master has failed more times than the beginner has even tried." We should be aware of the fact that we will fail our way to success. Before we even begin our journey, we need to make ourselves aware that there will be trials and tribulations. We will have to go through the hottest of hells, but we must have confidence that we will inevitably prevail.

The power of belief is an amazing feeling to harness if we choose to attract it and employ it in our favor. To believe is to be crystal clear about solving a Rubik's Cube. The more definite our vision, the more effective our belief will be. Merely believing in ourselves is the key to igniting our wildest imagination. These beliefs are how we perceive our world to be. Our beliefs are based on our values and philosophies. They also determine who we are as a person. Buddha teaches us that we are what we think about on a daily basis. Our thoughts are attractive. We become what we believe is true of us. If we think that we are successful, and that we have the power to impact the world positively, then that is what we will do. If we believe that there is not a better life for us, then we shall suffer in our belief system.

World-renowned speaker and personal development guru, Les Brown, mentioned in one of his speeches that the easiest thing he did was earning a million dollars. The hardest thing was to believe that it was possible for him to do so.

"The power of belief is the engine that runs the car of life." — DERRICK STANDIFER

The power of belief is the stepping-stone to creating miracles. As a native of Atlanta, I was on the wrong side of a miracle when the Falcons scored a 28–3 lead on the Patriots late into the third quarter of Super Bowl LI. The Patriots came back and eventually won that game. Everyone who was watching the game just *knew* that it was impossible for the Falcons to lose this game, even some Patriots fans began to admit defeat. However, the members on the Patriots team had faith, remained confident, and believed in their ability to create miracles. Even though that was a crushing loss, the miracle of that comeback was one that can inspire anyone to keep pushing and keep fighting even when all hope is ostensibly lost.

By definition, a miracle is an unexpected welcoming event that is not explicable by natural or scientific laws and is therefore considered to be the work of a divine agency. Prior to the miracle taking place, we must first welcome it into our existence. The Patriots' Super Bowl victory was indeed a miracle. The probability of the Patriots coming back to win was, according to some betting agencies, less than one percent. Some individuals who attempt to solve the Rubik's Cube would argue that their ability to solve it is a miracle, but the main thing is that they believe in miracles. These miracles are tapped into by searching for a belief much higher than ourselves.

"Successful people have fear, successful people have doubts, and successful people have worries. They just don't let these feelings stop them."
— T. HARV EKER

Many people believe that those who succeed were divinely chosen by God, while the rest are forced to sit on the sidelines and watch them shine with admiration. After reading many of their stories and dissecting what makes people successful, it is apparent that it is certain work habits that give them their desired lifestyle, not luck or some divine appointment. A combination of hard work and persistence, backed by belief, has launched them into greatness or at least an above average lifestyle.

These people fully believed in themselves and did not have backup plans. According to Will Smith, "If you have a Plan B, then your Plan A will never work." Stop having back up plans. Give all of your energy to Plan A. If you don't succeed, pick yourself back up knowing that you gave it your all and learn to be better in the process. Giving half effort will have Plan A, Plan B, Plan C, and all of the rest of your plans facing failure. Believe in yourself and the calling on your life. Give it your all or nothing at all.

INSIDE THE CUBE

1. What is one thing that you have always wanted to do, but did not believe that it was possible for you?

   _____

   _____

2. If needed, do you have people in your life who believe in you that you can borrow belief from?

   _____

   _____

3. Identify something that you once quit on, but you still wish that you had not.

   _____

   _____

4. Do you have backup plans? If yes, what is the main plan that you want to accomplish? Identify it and focus on that one thing.

   _____

   _____

5. How do you feel when you accomplish something that once made you afraid?

   _____

PART TWO

IT IS REPEATEDLY SAID THAT the secret of the rich is time management. However, these people have a burning belief in what to manage
their time on. There are overwhelming stories where people have been
written off as failures in life, yet they used other people's doubt to soar
to success. These individuals were able to accomplish the impossible
because they believed it was possible. As mentioned before, belief makes
miracles happen.

I did not realize how deep a hole I dug myself into when I first
attempted to re-enroll in school. I started out on this journey to earn my
bachelor's degree and complete what I had started; however, it was far
more difficult than expected. First, I tried to re-enroll back into Georgia
State University. I went into the admissions office, and they informed me
that I owed the University nearly $3,000 in reverse charges because I had
maxed out loans during the year and had not completed my coursework.
I still vividly remember the expression on the administrator's face with
whom I spoke. The look that he gave me let me know that I was an idiot
for dropping out, and the school would be an even bigger idiot if they
allowed me to re-enroll.

After a few tries, I set my sights on attending Kennesaw State
University, which was also another fail. I submitted my application for
the 2013–14 school year and I could not receive my transcript from GSU
because of my outstanding balance. I tried to maneuver different ways
around this, but to no avail. I thought that I could use my transcripts
from FAMU to enroll into KSU, but the University Systems of Georgia

flagged me. I lost another battle, but I was tenacious and determined to get back into school.

"Success consists of going from failure to failure without loss of enthusiasm." — WINSTON CHURCHILL

One thing that I have learned in life is that you will fail your way to success. "No," does not mean "NO." It either means not right now, that you have to find another way around the obstacle, or that you need to find someone who is able to assist you in reaching your destination. It takes determination even while people doubt you and when it seems as if you are attracted to failing.

Sometimes, taking a leap of faith is the best and only option. It forces you to take action, sometimes blindly, but it's better than taking no action at all. In many cases, we get stuck in life and don't know what course of action to take. When this happens, sometimes life will set a course for you.

I remember visiting Tallahassee for a poetry show where I was being featured. Meanwhile, I went to campus and sought the information that I needed to go back to school. I completed the re-enrollment process. As fate would have it, after I came back from Tallahassee, I was fired from my job as a server. The termination was a divine sign that my life's purpose was to serve in a different manner. I knew that I could substantially impact the world by finishing my education.

Instead of looking for another job, I subleased my apartment and sold my furniture. I took a leap of faith. My then wife, two dogs, Imhotep (pitbull) and Maya Angelou (chihuahua) and I moved back to

Tallahassee. We had little money, a clear destination, and a path burdened with obstacles, but we set out to accomplish this mission of finishing my degree. We did not know where we were going to live or what we were going to eat, but we had belief.

By believing in yourself, it encourages your friends to also believe in you; they will then support your dream. When we moved back to Tallahassee, we house hopped around with some of our friends. However, it got so unstable that we agreed that my wife should return home until we could at least find housing.

When I think about that leap of faith that we took, I think about how hard it is to make that journey into the unknown and the uncomfortable. I do understand how some people would not want to make that journey. It can be frightening. But believing in ourselves and taking that leap of faith is the only way to grow.

WAYS TO STRENGTHEN YOUR BELIEF

Of course, belief is the catalyst for all good things in our lives, but how do we strengthen our beliefs? These are a few key ways that I have researched and benefitted from by staying disciplined and following through on these steps.

SEE YOURSELF AS A SOLVER OF THE RUBIK'S CUBE VISUALIZATION

Belief is the first step to solving the Rubik's Cube, and that belief has to be concise. You have to first see yourself as a solver of the Rubik's Cube. To strengthen our beliefs, we must visualize our ideas, and activate our reticular activating system (RAS) to magnetize our goals.

Our RAS serves as a goal finder; it finds what we desire and what is most important to us. We can train our minds into strengthening our beliefs. There are several ways to accomplish such training of the mind for the progress of life. Decide which of the following methods align with you or utilize them all. The more you train your mind, the stronger it will become.

On Jack Canfield's blog, he mentions that visualization allows four essential things, which include:

1. *It activates your creative subconscious*, which will generate creative ideas to achieve your goals.

2. *It programs your brain* to promptly recognize the resources you will need to achieve your dreams.

3. *It activates the Law of Attraction*, thereby bringing into your life the people, resources, and circumstances you will need to achieve your goals.

4. *It builds your internal motivation* to take the necessary actions to achieve your dreams.

VISION BOARDS

Another way to enhance your belief system is to create a vision board; desirably some place where you will see it every day. A vision board is used to concentrate our focus on specific desires of whoever we aspire to be or whatever we seek to attain in life.

Where there is no vision, there is no hope.
— GEORGE WASHINGTON CARVER

Visualizing our desires attracts them to us. Creating a vision board evokes joy and excitement about accomplishing our goals. What is written is real, therefore, only write or paste things on your vision board that you intend to manifest. Setting goals is an acute priority, but how do we maintain focus on a preferred goal and see it every single day? Having a goal list is also a great way to get started, but when the goal is not readily available or if it's hidden in the pages of your goal book, how do you visualize what it is that you want? Creating vision boards is an excellent way of overcoming this.

Oftentimes, people attend vision board parties, and the environment is one that fosters growth and prosperity. Successful people set goals; the fastest way to become successful is to surround yourself with other successful people. This forces us to focus on our objectives regularly. It holds us accountable. How can we look at our goals every day, and not strive for them? The direction is there; all we have to do is take the first step along the journey.

> **LIFE IS ABOUT FALLING SO DEEPLY IN LOVE WITH YOURSELF THAT YOU DON'T CARE WHAT OTHERS THINK ABOUT YOU.**

AFFIRMATIONS

Affirmations are positive statements that are intended to be repeated until they are impressed upon the subconscious mind. These statements are directly related to our chosen intentions. After repeating them multiple times a day, our minds begin to internalize them. As a result, our minds work much harder to make our affirmations come true. Many people repeat conflicting statements to themselves more so than positive ones. When we make mistakes, we beat ourselves up with degrading comments such as, "I'm so stupid." Consequently, we create adverse situations in our lives. Life and death are in the power of the tongue.

> **"You will be a failure until you impress the subconscious with the conviction you are a success. This is done by making an affirmation which 'clicks.'"**
> **— FLORENCE SCOVEL SHINN**

Thoughts become words, words become actions, actions become habits, and habits define who we are. The words that we tell ourselves determine the foundation of our success or our future. If we tell ourselves that we cannot solve the Rubik's Cube, then that will become true, unless we shift our mindset. Everyone who is able to solve the Rubik's Cube picks it up and tells themselves, "I can solve the Rubik's Cube." Our minds are a magnet to words, and it attracts what we seek out, what we repeat to ourselves, and what it is that we really want. Only think what you want to attract.

I recall the first time that I began running with my accountability partner, who is a regular runner. I told myself that I wanted to keep up with his pace and mileage. It was a pride thing. I couldn't just let him outrun me. I knew that I could run a mile or two, and that was pushing it.

After we were done, we had run a little over four miles. I honestly couldn't believe it. During the run, I kept telling myself, "Derrick, you got this, you are strong." These positive affirmations gave me the strength to strive harder. Under any other circumstances, I would not have been able to keep going, but telling myself that I had to keep up is what made me conquer those beliefs.

BE YOUR OWN BEST FRIEND

Bernie Mac had a quote that completely revolutionized the way that I felt about myself. Someone once told him, "Bernie, I don't like you!" His response was genius. He said, "I don't care if you like me, I like me."

When you are chasing your dreams, some people will make it their mission to highlight your flaws or choose to judge you negatively. How other people feel about you has nothing to do with your success. If someone decides to take energy away from their goals to focus on yours, then you let them do it, but do not engage with them. People will talk about you for the rest of your life, especially if you are successful. Let them give you free publicity.

Life is not about getting people to like you. Life is about falling so deeply in love with yourself that you don't care what others think about you. I've seen many people lose their temper, job, or even life over how someone felt about them. To be successful, you have to develop a tough-ness about yourself that isn't easily broken by insults. Over time, I got used to the insults and embraced being an outcast. I learned to accept that not everyone will like me, and that was ok because I would much rather have four quarters than one hundred pennies.

"I don't care if you like me, I like me."
— BERNIE MAC

YOU DON'T HAVE TO BE SMART TO SOLVE THE RUBIK'S CUBE

A huge misconception about solving the Rubik's Cube is that you have to be a natural-born genius. All people are natural-born geniuses. Sadly, many of us do not take the time to develop what we are naturally good at, so we take our gifts and talents to the grave. Not everyone steps into their greatness, but everyone is a genius in their realm. In the same manner that Albert Einstein was a genius of his field, Muhammad Ali was a boxing genius. All people are born intelligent, and each of these people can solve the Rubik's Cube inside of them.

"You don't have to be a genius or a visionary or even a college graduate to be successful. You just need a framework and a dream."
— MICHAEL DELL

When I first began teaching people how to solve the Rubik's Cube, it was to students, ages 9–14. Many of the students were still learning how to read; however, they comprehended colors. Color recognition is the primary skill that you need to be able to solve the Rubik's Cube. Many people overcomplicate the Rubik's Cube and intimidate others with algorithms. I don't know anything about an algorithm, but I do know that all the reds should go together. We sometimes overcomplicate what it is that we desire in life.

INSIDE THE CUBE

1. What are your best skills? Identify things that you are naturally good at (speaking, dancing, math).

   _____

   _____

2. What are things that you like doing that make you feel good about yourself?

   _____

   _____

3. What are your biggest character strengths (brave, honest, kind)?

   _____

   _____

4. What do you value most in life?

   _____

   _____

5. Where are your favorite places to be in the world?

   _____

   _____

STEP TWO
SOLVE YOUR CROSS

THE NEXT STEP TO SOLVING the Rubik's Cube is solving your cross. Visually, solving your cross means to solve the central squares horizontally and vertically. It will look like a plus sign or a cross. In life, solving your cross means defining your *why*. Every successful person has a personal and unwavering "why," which serves as their motivation to reach extraordinary achievements. There are a myriad of trials and tribulations that can break a person who has not established a compelling "why."

A cemented "why" makes it easier to rebound when life knocks you down, and in this journey of life, you will be knocked down by life's brutal punches. Sylvester Stallone, Rocky Balboa, a boxer in the 2006 film, stated that, "It's not about how hard you get hit, it's about how hard you get hit and keep on moving." In life, everyone experiences a multitude of mountain peaks and valleys. We appreciate the mountain peaks, but despise the valleys.

"He who has a why can endure any how."
— FRIEDRICH NIETZSCHE

If you look at the image, you will notice that the cross resembles a plus sign. The plus sign operates as your "personal charger" and keeps you stimulated to solve the entire puzzle. In life, our motivation battery *will* become drained, and we will need a "personal charger" to re-energize our energy levels to peak performance. Like the plus sign, your "why" is your charger.

A relentless "why" helps you to remain focused on your goals, dreams, and aspirations without being hindered by distractions. However, when we are chasing success, we will encounter obstacles along the way, but we must not allow them to sway us from our path. We live in a world where miscellaneous things are constantly vying for our attention.

Television, social media, and even spending time with friends are all the things that can steal away from our future if we are not careful. With a strong "why" ingrained, we can ask ourselves, "Does this help us achieve our desired goal, or is it a distraction?" Your "why" must be strong enough to make you put down your cell phone and chase your dreams. Your "why" must make you turn off the television, especially if you are not where you want to be in life. If you are not where you desire to be in life, then you do not have time to indulge in such frivolous entertainment.

In addition to staying focused, creating an intense "why" will give you the courage to face fears and overcome obstacles that would have otherwise ended your journey before you even got started. There are numerous accounts where people have accomplished the seemingly impossible because their "why" pushed them to greatness.

In the movie, *Cinderella Man*, Russell Crowe played the role of James Braddock, a boxer who was widely considered one of the greatest fighters of his time before the Great Depression. After suffering from a severe hand injury, he was forced to quit boxing and work on docking ships. Like many families during the Great Depression, he and his family battled difficult times. They endured illness, lack of food, and the embarrassment of having to beg for money. There was one scene where they did not have enough milk to feed the children, and his wife had to supplement the milk with water. I'm sure this incident remained planted in his mind, as it would any father who is struggling to provide for his family.

One day he was offered an opportunity to fight a title contender. Against all the odds, he ended up knocking out his opponent, which opened the door for more fights. He then went on a winning streak deeming him a true Cinderella story. During an interview, he was asked, "What are you fighting for?" He responded, "I'm fighting for milk." His "why" was strengthened when he had to take care of his family, by any means necessary. He made a way to keep his family together and provide for them. This story is an amazing demonstration of persevering through the darkest of times.

"Everything negative—pressure, challenges— is all an opportunity for me to rise." — KOBE BRYANT

The story of Buster Douglas is another example of the power of having a fortified "why." Douglas is a boxing legend who gained world fame for being the victor in one of the intense upsets in boxing history. He shockingly knocked out Mike Tyson in the 10th round of the fight. Douglas received his motivation two days before the match while on his mother's deathbed as she told him that she believed he could beat the undefeated Mike Tyson. She died shortly after her prognostication.

Mike Tyson had not lost a fight in all of his 37 contests and expected to easily defeat Douglas so that he could defend his title against Evander Holyfield. However, Douglas had different plans. At that time, Tyson was by far the greatest boxer on the planet, and no one in their right mind would have chosen Douglas to win this fight. But, if your mother was on her deathbed, and she informed you that you were going to accomplish a major feat, wouldn't you make it your God-given mission to make it happen?

His mother resonated with him throughout the fight and motivated him to endure the punishing punches of Tyson. Douglas fought valiantly, however, in the 8th round, Tyson ended up catching him with a "good shot." Douglas rebounded by dominating the 9th round, and in the 10th, he knocked out Mike Tyson with what he called "four terrific shots." The "four terrific shots" caused Tyson to fail to recover in time for the count. Douglas had accomplished the impossible and surprised the world, all due to the strength of his "why."

In the 2017 NFL Draft, former UCLA Defensive End, Takkarist McKinley, emphasized extreme passion for his "why," which was his grandmother. The Atlanta Falcons selected McKinley with the 26th overall pick. During his interview, he delivered a heartfelt speech about his feelings experienced when his grandmother passed away. As his name was called, he brought on stage a picture of his grandmother, Myrtle Collins. McKinley was abandoned by his mother when he was just five years old, and he never met his father. Thus, Myrtle Collins raised the young boy. To take care of the bills, they collected cans and sold them at recycling centers.

His "why" for getting drafted was developed in 2011 after he rushed to the hospital to visit his grandmother, who was lying on her deathbed after suffering from several strokes. At that moment, he promised his grandmother that he would make it out of the tough neighborhood of Richmond, California, play Division 1 football, and eventually play in the NFL. She died shortly after he made his promise. He stated, "I probably wouldn't be sitting here talking to you guys if I didn't make that promise." McKinley's story highlights what it means to combine immense talent with a secure "why." He declared, "That's what fuels me. That's why I play how I play and why I act how I act. When I got on stage, there was just a bunch of emotion that just kind of flowed out. The promise is complete, but as far as what I want to accomplish, it's just the beginning. But that promise I made to her means everything."

I had to solve my cross to make improvements in my own personal life. I had several "whys," some were deep, meaningful, and profound; others were ignorant and petty.

My most motivating "why" are my children. They are the real reason why I wake up early and why I hustle as hard as I do. They are the reason why this book is published. I declared to myself that if I quit, then I am giving my children reason to quit.

In my opinion, there is no more significant motivation than knowing that you have mouths to feed other than your own. When my daughter was born, her mother and I could have been featured on the TV show *I Didn't Know I Was Pregnant*. After testing positive for a pregnancy test, we made an appointment to go to the doctor. I thought that the doctor was crazy because he told us that my wife was 28 weeks pregnant. I thought there was no way that this doctor is competent. Our daughter, Ayana, was in a hurry to get into the world. She was born six weeks premature due to a condition that is known as preeclampsia, at 4 pounds 5 ounces.

When I first laid eyes on her, I immediately knew it was my responsibility to establish a strong foundation for my daughter to build upon for the rest of her life. Now, as I watch her grow and develop a personality of her own, she amazes me more than I ever thought was possible. I must show her good qualities of a man. She will pay attention to me even when I think that she is not, so I must uphold a standard of excellence at all times. I must act by what I want my daughter to be exposed to as a man.

Now that my son is born, that feeling of deep love has doubled. In the same manner that my daughter will learn what a man should be from me, my son will learn what manhood is from me. Therefore, I must uphold the honor of teaching my son as my life's highest priority, just as I do my daughter.

As a product of a single mother, I witnessed my mom travel back and forth to work on public transportation. She worked twelve-hour shifts and raised three children who didn't appreciate her efforts until we had children and she passed away. My mother is another prominent "why" that fuels me towards success. She was indeed a talented, hard-working woman, and sacrificed to ensure that I can live a better quality of life. Since her transition, I honor her legacy and her hardworking nature in her death.

"The greatest revenge is massive success!"
— FRANK SINATRA

Another "why" that I have is one that is petty. However, I believe that sometimes we need dragons to fight to add fire to our motivation. When I was in school, I was bullied a lot. My mom couldn't afford to buy expensive clothes, so I was teased because of my wardrobe. I started going to Goodwill to buy blazers and button-down shirts. They referred to me as "Kanye East," the fake version of Kanye West because I imitated his style.

On top of that, I had crooked teeth; I was the laughing stock of all the kids. I was called every name in the book. For every joke that was made about teeth, I was on the receiving end of the insults. They called me everything from "Yuck Mouth" to "Gangsta Grillz." My line name when I pledged Alpha Phi Omega was "Gator Mouth." Someone in school once said, "Derrick, it looks like somebody took your teeth, shook them up, and threw them back in your mouth."

At first, I felt horrible for being bullied and picked on all the time. However, sometimes while the bad is happening, it is difficult to see the benefits that the pain creates. These experiences made me develop a "tough skin." Over time, their jokes did not bother me as they once did. As a matter of fact, I learned to laugh at the remarks myself. I appreciated the development and the mental toughness that enabled me to ignore their jokes. At the time, I had to find a reason to justify my feelings, and I did. My peers' jokes about me served as a primary reason to continue to pursue success. I assured myself that I would be the guy that they would regret making fun of.

A prominent motivating factor for me to relentlessly chase success was the first time I met my former father-in-law. My former wife was graduating, and I was meeting her parents for the very first time. After graduation, everyone wanted to go out to eat, but we did not make reservations. If you have ever been to Tallahassee during graduation weekend, then you know that the city is packed, and there are hour-long waits at every restaurant. We ended up at a pizza place. When we met her father and uncle there, her dad asked to speak to me privately outside. I took a deep breath and tried to prepare myself for what was about to happen. In my mind, I pictured the scene from *Bad Boys 2* when Martin Lawrence and Will Smith first met Martin's daughter's boyfriend, and they almost made him urinate in his pants.

When we got outside, they cornered me and started cursing me out because we were eating at a pizza restaurant. Her uncle said, "Boy, I make 50k a year, does it look like I want to eat some *DAMN* pizza?" In my head, I thought, "All you can afford is some *DAMN* pizza." They were asking me millions of questions and made me feel horrible about my existence. (Now, I'm thinking to myself that I'm going to do the same thing to my daughter's boyfriend.)

He asked me what I did to earn money; I replied that I waited tables and was a poet. Right after the words left my mouth, a homeless man came up to us and recited a poem. Jasmine's dad looked at me and said, "That's gonna be your ass talking about being a damn poet." By the time we made it back to the pizzeria, her father had "torn me a new ass," as my mother would say. He told me that he had money set aside for his daughter to come back home. I couldn't be upset with him because I was doing absolutely nothing with my life. Nevertheless, I was determined to prove him wrong. I would be able to take care of us and provide for his daughter.

It is astounding how we can turn our pains into the most substantial reasons for why we must become successful. It doesn't matter where we get the drive and motivation from, all that matters is that we understand where we are going and what we hope to gain from traveling there. Our "why" makes us do things that we typically wouldn't do if it were not involved. Sometimes, we need that extra push to solve our cross.

INSIDE THE CUBE

1. Who are people in your life that you want to make proud?

   _____

   _____

2. Sometimes we need a dragon to slay. Who are people who told you that you were going to be a failure at life or who doubted you?

   _____

   _____

3. How do you want to be remembered by your family and loved ones?

   _____

   _____

4. What excuses have you been using to justify why not having your goals?

   _____

   _____

5. What do you need to accomplish your goals? How can you get it?

   _____

   _____

STEP THREE
FILL IN YOUR CORNERS

PART ONE

BELIEF IN YOURSELF AND SOLVING your cross will lead you to the next step of conquering the Rubik's Cube: filling in your corners. Pertaining to the Rubik's Cube, you will need to make sure that the corners are lined up with the same color. In life, filling in your corners merely means to surround yourself with people who will push and motivate you to a new level. Filling in your corners also consists of listening to motivational messages on a daily basis. These concepts are vital and foundational, especially if you are attempting to learn to solve the Rubik's Cube inside of yourself.

If you live in a positive environment that consists of people encouraging you and providing support, then you will most likely develop into a person who reflects such values. On the contrary, if you live in a negative environment filled with negative people who complain about their problems, but never work toward changing their situation, then you have a higher chance of becoming a person who reflects those values.

THE POWER OF MENTORS

I was raised in a negative community that was detrimental to my personal development. From first-hand experience, I can tell you that growing up poor can set a child back drastically from reaching their full potential. My mother dropped out of school in the tenth grade and was a single parent of three boys. Nevertheless, she did the best she could to raise us despite her limited resources. I still can't believe that she worked twelve-hour shifts, five days a week and rode the bus almost two hours to and from work. My brothers and I grew up in the impoverished sections of Atlanta, Georgia. We lived in neighborhoods that were poverty stricken, where drug use was rampant and the school systems were of low quality.

According to the statistics, I should have been a high school dropout just like my mother and brothers. That would have been my trajectory, and I would have continued the cycle of not completing anything if someone had not made me believe that I could do more with my life. I look at my brothers, who are both smart, but did not have the same opportunities that I had. They did not have people in their lives who believed in them. I am a product of great mentors and role models who believed in me, and I strove to meet their expectations. Those experiences have caused me to admire the words of Johann Wolfgang von Goethe, "Look at a man the way he is, and he only becomes worse, but look at him as if he were what he could be, then he becomes what he should be."

It was, and still is, a fortunate blessing to have mentors and role models who exposed me to more nurturing environments. They believed in me and supported me throughout my journey, and I wanted to make them proud. One of the greatest motivating emotions that we can witness is a child who wants to make their parents and mentors proud. These people made me work harder when I thought about them. So many of them invested in me, and the only thing that they have asked of me is to pay it forward. I work hard with the mindset that I must establish myself so that I can pay it forward to another child or individual who is full of potential.

I keep in contact with these people as often as I can. In many cases, they served as surrogate parents to me. These were mainly former teachers, who I just happened to keep in contact with throughout the years. In return, they always spoke words of life and encouragement over me. They were my fountains of replenishment when I needed to be uplifted. Whenever I messed up, they were always there to reprimand me while also offering tough

JOHANN WOLFGANG VON GOETHE, "LOOK AT A MAN THE WAY HE IS, AND HE ONLY BECOMES WORSE, BUT LOOK AT HIM AS IF HE WERE WHAT HE COULD BE, THEN HE BECOMES WHAT HE SHOULD BE."

love and comfort. Even when I needed someone to grieve with, they made themselves available. People who love and support you unconditionally help you create an urgency toward success. More times than not, we will do things for other people that we would not do for ourselves.

Surround yourself with people who make you want to improve in all areas of life. People who love you will get under your skin and become aggravating. You must remember that the superficial annoyance is stemming from a deep source of love. Wise people give wise words of advice. Make it a mission to listen.

Have you ever noticed that when you make yourself a part of a particular group, you all begin to develop certain traits? These similar interests were not initially designed as such. At first, everyone entered the circle of friendship with their interests and hobbies. However, over time, each person began to influence each other minutely.

Over an extended period, we grow accustomed to our friends and have even adopted some of their habits, preferences, and likings. No matter how hard we try to prevent this phenomenon, these changes are inevitable. Why? We are an average of our closest friends.

The aspect of us rubbing off on our friends is interrelated with so many other areas of life. If one were interested in getting sick, then they would try and find themselves in the presence of sick people. If you would like to become successful, the quickest way of doing so is to hang out with successful people. Because successful people are fully aware that they are who they surround themselves with, they are meticulous about who can join their circle of influence.

If we surround ourselves with 10's and high-quality people, we too are most likely classified as a 10 or a high-quality person, or at least one in the making. It is essential that we are conscious of the goals of our associates. Thus, if we want to change ourselves, then we must change the people around us. I don't mean by convincing them to have goals, dreams, and aspirations, I mean by excluding them from your inner circle. It takes sacrifice if you want to become successful. If you can't make the sacrifices, then you don't want to become successful. If you can't change the people around you, then you are not willing to improve yourself.

BENEFITS OF HAVING GREAT QUALITY FRIENDS

Some people are not aware of the importance of having quality friends in their inner circle. Choosing your friends is a life or death decision. The moment you decide that you will allow people into your life, you also allow their traits and desires to become yours. Proverbs 13:20 states, "He who walks with wise men will be wise, but the companion of fools will suffer harm." Deductive reasoning states that we are an average of the people who we hang around the most. As a matter of fact, your friends play a serious role in your decision-making skills. We usually seek out our top friends for information and guidance. Do you want your advice coming from a person who is grounded in success, or one who is rooted in failure? Assess your closest friends and answer the question.

Our friends build us up, keep us motivated and inspired. True friends serve the role of a coach in your corner. At times, we cannot see the skills inside of us, but our friends can. Sometimes we cannot see what's in the picture; therefore, we must rely on a trusted friend who will stand outside of the frame and observe us. A genuine friend gives us honest, critical feedback on areas in which we need to grow, but from an outside perspective.

When you embark upon a journey of filling your inner circle with only quality people, then you block out negative influences by default. I like to call it weed pulling. If you are even minutely familiar with farming, then you know that where there are plants, there are also weeds. We must continuously pull and uproot our weeds because they abate nutrients from the plant.

In our lives, the weeds represent any aspect of negativity that will bring us down and diminish our nutrients. People who gossip about others are weeds that need to be removed from your garden. People who are always down, sad, and aggravated are weeds that need to be withdrawn from your life. Don't invite anyone in your circle who will steal your nutrients.

Since the information we input in our brains strongly affects our behaviors, it would behoove us to be aware of our environment. Successful people are cognizant of the main reason they are successful: it is due to the company that they keep. We should seek out high performers if we plan to be successful. High performing people know that they must associate with other like-minded individuals or people who are working toward becoming a top performer. If not, they will soon lose their status of success.

Dr. Dennis Kimbro, a professor and motivational speaker from Atlanta, GA, spoke powerful words when he said, "If you are the smartest person in your group, then you need to find yourself a new group." Those we choose to associate with should make us better, and if they don't, then we are being brought down by default.

If you are the smartest person in your circle, then you are feeding your ego instead of nurturing your future success. As the most intelligent person in the room, you will become the one who everyone sees as the go-to guy for information, but that makes you complacent with a glowing smile on your face. What motivation do you have to get better and to grow? How will you climb the ladder of success if you believe that you are already at the top?

"You will only ever be as great as the people you surround yourself with so be brave enough to let go of those who keep bringing you down."
— DERRICK STANDIFER

HOW CAN A NEW CIRCLE OF FRIENDS MAKE US BETTER?

Upon my return to FAMU, the first thing I decided to change was who I would spend time with during my matriculation. Choosing my peers was a critical step if I was to change my life. Instead of sitting at the back of the classroom where the students paid little to no attention to their professors, I sat on the front row. You can almost guarantee that those sitting on the front row make the highest grades. I became their friends, and we studied tirelessly together. We collectively went to our professors' office often to check for understanding. We did this in every class. We were all committed to the cause. My first semester back I earned five A's and only one C.

The next semester, I continued the same habits of surrounding myself with people who were success driven. That summer semester was the last semester that I needed to graduate and complete my degree. I was able to finish strong and complete what I had started. My final semester culminated with two A's and one C.

Going back to school was far more difficult than when I first enrolled because I took a lot of time away from school. I had to re-acclimate to the academic environment. The transition was made easier when I befriended people who were determined to earn high grades in class. As we studied, I picked up some of their scholarly habits. They made sense of some of the concepts that were confusing to me. I became mostly an A student because of my associations.

WHEN YOU HAVE GOOD FRIENDS, YOU MUST ALSO BE A GOOD FRIEND

While it is essential to have good friends in our circle of influence, we must remember that we have to be a great friend as well. In the same way that we do not want parasitic people draining us of our energy, it is crucial to avoid draining other people.

Motivate and inspire your friends to realize the greatness that's inside of them. When you encourage other people to let their light shine bright, your light gets brighter as well.

QUALITY VS. QUANTITY

Humans are social beings and need human interaction. Because the need for human interaction is so vital, some places consider solitary confinement as torture. There is a need-based factor to interact with other people. It is important to make and maintain healthy friendships; however, it is pertinent to never sacrifice the quality of your friends for the number of friends. In a day and age where we find value in the number of Facebook friends and followers on social media, it can be easy to lose track of the number of friends that we really have.

Be friendly and make more friends. Porter Gale once said, "Your net worth lies in your network." Remember to seek out quality friends. Don't settle for someone with no values just for the sake of having a friend. It is not worth the destruction that poor-quality friends can cause in your life.

Plato, the Greek philosopher, beautifully described why we need quality friends. He said, "People are like dirt. They can either nourish you and help you grow as a person, or they can stunt your growth and make you wilt and die."

Joining a mastermind group is an exceptional way to surround your-self with people who will elevate you and push you to take life to the next level. In 2016, I formed a mastermind group with some amazing brothers all in their respective ways. We utilized the book, *Think and Grow Rich,* by Napoleon Hill to model the operations format.

Over time, we grew to become brothers and our accountability to each other was great. We took an "all for one and one for all" approach to our mastermind. As a result, everyone reached another level. In fact, one of our members quit his job and became a full-time entrepreneur. Two of our members were already entrepreneurs and had started an award-winning company that has been featured in several acclaimed magazines, including the front page of Ebony. Our commitment to each other made us grow as individuals.

Everyone was a beast in their own right, and it enabled us to make each other better through different lenses. We pushed one another out of the dark cave of laziness and procrastination, and into the light of a focused work ethic and a disciplined lifestyle. It is evident that our habits rubbed off on one another. We rooted for each other, made each other better, and gave pep talks whenever we lost focus.

LISTENING TO MOTIVATIONAL MESSAGES

Instead of listening to music filled with negativity, we should replace it with motivational messages. Our minds are like gardens and what we put into our minds are the seeds. If we feed our minds grains of nutrition, value, and substance, then we will produce actions of value and substance. What we listen to and watch are definite factors in who we become.

After going back to school, I approached my matriculation with a brand-new mindset, and I had to be aware of what I was putting into my conscience. I began to go to the library, and when it was time to do research or write an assignment, I would listen to motivational speeches on YouTube and play them while I was writing. This changed the work environment for me.

It is harder to lose focus when you have a speaker playing in your ear encouraging you to stay focused and not to quit. Every day while studying in the library, I had Les Brown, Zig Ziglar, and Jim Rohn playing in my ear. It quickly became part of my routine and I started seeing the results. I never knew what the newest music was because I only listened to motivational speeches. They became addictive because their principles worked. I completely immersed myself in positive, motivating speeches. When I was riding the bus, I had my speeches playing. When I finally got a car, all I listened to were speeches. People would get in my car and ask, "Do you have any music that we can listen to?" I did, but I preferred my speeches.

There is music that we can listen to in order to receive our dose of positivity. Positive music isn't mainstream, so you have to do some searching to find artists that you like. At first, listening to motivational speeches might seem weird and may be something that you don't want to do. However, over time, you will get accustomed to it and find music or speeches that work for you.

Surrounding yourself with positive people who will elevate you is a fundamental factor in filling in your corners. To ensure a strong hold on your mind, you must also make it a mission to listen to positive audio and watch uplifting visuals daily. Both have profound effects on how we develop into who we are destined to be.

INSIDE THE CUBE

1. Who are positive influences in your life?

   _____

   _____

2. Who are your favorite motivational speakers or authors?

   _____

   _____

3. Who are the people that you look up to?

   _____

   _____

4. Who are the greatest people who do what you want to do?

   _____

   _____

5. What are the positive traits you desire your friends to have that will also help you?

   _____

   _____

PART TWO

JUST AS SURROUNDING YOURSELF WITH positive people is critical to staying positive, so is ensuring that negative people are kept out of your inner circle as much as possible in ensuring the success of maintaining a positive mindset. Do not limit your thinking to people only. There are many situations in our world that stir up the negative and spoil our airspace.

KEEPING YOUR CORNERS STRONG

Zig Ziglar has a saying that I have now made a part of my makeup. He proclaims, "You are what you are and you are where you are because of what has gone into your mind. You change what you are and you change where you are by changing what goes into your mind."

Jim Rohn tells us that his teacher taught him to, "Everyday stand guard at the door of your mind." Your mind is your most valuable asset when it comes to chasing success.

SOMETIMES WE HAVE TO CUT OUR FRIENDS LOOSE

In our journey of changing the people who are around us, we may sometimes find ourselves in a predicament where we may have to lose friends who we once thought would be lifelong companions. Although it may be hurtful, it is important to realize that what we think is good for us can hurt us as well. If we have toxic friends in our lives, we have to ask ourselves the simple question, "Do I want to be great or do I want this friendship?" Jim Rohn famously asked a question, "What if our best friend, even by accident, dropped strychnine in our coffee?" Strychnine is a poisonous substance that will kill you if consumed. Now, we wouldn't approve of our friends killing us even if it was by accident.

When I first moved to Tallahassee to attend the illustrious FAMU, I was discovering who I wanted to be. I didn't understand the concept of "you are who you associate with." I made some wonderful friends, but they did not make school a top priority. I saw many days and nights when I chose to hang out rather than study. As a result, my grades dropped. Eventually, I dropped out of FAMU.

I then decided to enroll at GSU, where I thought that I was going to get my act together. Even then, I found myself surrounded by brilliant minds who were all against formal education. I soon adopted their same sentiments. Your friends must have overlapping beliefs if you want to become successful. If you believe that school is your key, but your friends believe that crime and drugs are their keys, then your friends will bring you down to their mentality.

When I decided to go back to school, I realized that I had to go on a hiatus from the thoughts and beliefs that did not align with my desired results. My primary mission was to obtain a degree. To accomplish that mission, I had to put

MAKE IT YOUR DUTY TO CONSTANTLY SEEK OUT THE GOOD AND ELIMINATE THE BAD

people in my inner circle who also had the same purpose. If I chose to do the opposite, then my journey to graduation would have been a lot more difficult or nonexistent. Think about it as taking a walk with someone.

On this walk, one of two things will happen. One of you will slow down or speed up to match the pace of the other walker. Be cautious of who you choose to walk with in life. They could either slow you down on your journey or speed you up.

TYPES OF PEOPLE TO AVOID

I know that in a perfect world we befriend everyone who we encounter. Unfortunately, this world is far from perfect, and there are people that we should avoid. Sometimes it is difficult to dodge certain people, but again, ask yourself the question, "Do I want the lifestyle of the person that I am spending my time with?" If the answer is no, then abstain yourself from them before you end up with their lifestyle. In our journey of learning how to solve our own Rubik's Cube, we must learn how to prevent interaction with certain people.

AVOID PEOPLE WHO ARE NEGATIVE ON SOCIAL MEDIA

If you ever logged onto Facebook or Instagram, you may notice there is always a person who continually makes dramatic posts. Even though these people are not in our physical space, seeing their comments can be equally damaging. Every time I see negative posts, gossip or anything that will do more harm than good to my psyche, I delete that person. Allow the unfollow button to become your friend.

AVOID PARASITES

In science, a parasite is a living organism that feeds on another organism and provides no advantages to the host. There are sometimes parasitic people in our lives who only feed on us and give no benefit. Extinguish these people out of your life before they drain your resources, time, and energy with nothing in return.

AVOID NEGATIVE PEOPLE AT THE WORKPLACE/SCHOOL

Some places are harder to avoid certain types of people. At a job, you can't completely ignore your micromanaging boss or that co-worker who won't stop telling you about all of their downfalls. Treat these people with respect and kindness, but treat them as associates. If negative people invite you out for an after-hour drink, politely turn their offer down. If they think that you are rude, then consider that the price for keeping the energy drainers out of your life. It is important not to worry much about how negative people view you. Do not let it make you feel guilty.

AVOID PEOPLE WHO ARE ALWAYS THE "VICTIM"

I wish I had received this advice a few years ago when I wanted to tell everyone about the valleys that I was experiencing. I felt the need to tell my sad, suck-up story to anybody who would listen. I thought that making people feel bad about my situation would help my situation. However, all it did was make me focus more on the situation. Doubtless to say, people don't care about your problems. Everyone has personal problems to deal with, and don't want to waste energy focusing on your issues.

NEGATIVE MUSIC

Now, I completely understand what my parents felt like when they complained about the music that I grew up listening to and admiring. I hope that a trend of positive, uplifting and respectful rap music would re-emerge and take over from what today's youth refer to as music. If you were to look up the lyrics of the top ten rap songs that are on the radio, you would realize that the lyrics promote drug usage, violence, disrespect of women and more. The songs are of good quality; the beats are electrifying, the lyrics are witty, but the topics are damaging. I understand the notion of writing about life and what you experience, but we have to break that narrative to impact our youth positively. These messages of violence and inferiority are drilled into our children, which make them adopt these principles for their lives.

Why can't our hip-hop stars write on topics of encouragement and positivity? Why can't we make music of how we plan to build up ourselves in ways that also make us proud? Unfortunately, I have realized that negativity sells. We are being programmed to see negativity as the norm. What would the value of our lives be if we started taking back our minds? What if we reprogram ourselves to the beauty, positivity, and success in life? It would drastically change this world's trajectory for the better.

AVOID NEGATIVE MEDIA

Avoiding negative media can be counterintuitive to what we are taught during our adolescence, but watching the news does way more harm than it does good. I am aware that stories are happening throughout the world that we might need to be cognizant of, but the negative stories filled with crime and violence are not stories that we should consume regularly. We can definitely afford to leave those where they are.

MENTAL AND PHYSICAL DAMAGE INCURRED BY WATCHING THE NEWS

Markham Heid, a writer for *Time Magazine*, wrote a mind-opening article about the dangers of watching the news. He argued that the news causes anxiety, stress, and even sleep loss to those who view it, especially with the rise of bystander recordings and social media.

Every day, people are capable of uploading news content via their social media accounts. Sadly, the negative news content attracts the most attention. He goes on to say that news channels can even cause those who watch it physical pain, such as inflammation associated with rheumatoid arthritis, cardiovascular disease, and other serious health concerns.

If the news is damaging to our bodies and minds, then why do so many people revert to watching the news? According to the article, and Loretta Breuning, a former professor of Management at the University of California, "The human brain is attracted to troubling information because it's programmed to detect threats, not to overlook them. This can make it hard for us to ignore the negatives and seek out the positives around us," she says, "Our brain is predisposed to go negative, and the news we consume reflects this."

News channels should keep us abreast of what is going on in the world so that we can prepare for opportunity instead of tragedy. News today encourages us to prepare for war, killings, and rapes.

It is not too often that we hear about the long-lasting wedding anniversaries, or love and peace. We have become so accustomed to the negativity in life that we fail to notice the beauty. News channels report happenings in the world, and people genuinely believe that this information is of value. Poet, Ralph Waldo Emerson, teaches us that, "There are many things of which a wise man might wish to be ignorant."

While watching the news, we should ask ourselves the question, "Will this information make me better, enhance my life, or put me in a positive mind frame? Or is this destructive and will put me in a worrisome state of mind?"

Albert Einstein affirmed, "The most important decision a man will ever make is whether he lives in a friendly universe." If one of the most brilliant minds to walk this planet acknowledged the importance of immersing ourselves in a positive environment, then we must listen.

People thrive in environments where they are uplifted, motivated, and empowered. The more we foster this environment, the more the environment will foster us. Make it your duty to constantly seek out the good and eliminate the bad. Even the smallest of poison can damage our health. The smallest amount of negative thinking can be damaging to our success and ambitions.

Choose your input of people and ideas wisely; this may be the essential decision that you can make in your life. Charlie Jones, a world-renowned motivational speaker, said, "In five years we will be the same person except for the books that we read and the friends that we make."

Choose wisely.

INSIDE THE CUBE

1. What do you consider to be negative influences in your life?

   _____

   _____

2. Can you identify those people in your life who fall under the
   categories of those to avoid?

   _____

   _____

3. What music do you listen to that delivers negative messages?

   _____

   _____

4. Do you watch any TV programs that you consider to be
   negative? Why?

   _____

   _____

5. What keeps you from breaking free from the effects of negativity
   in your life?

   _____

   _____

STEP FOUR
TAKE IT TO THE NEXT LEVEL

AFTER WE BELIEVE, SOLVE OUR cross, and fill in our corners, we approach the fourth step of solving the Rubik's Cube, which is to take it to the next level. Taking it to the next level is a metaphor for continuing to expand and improve in life.

Elevation is essential, not only for success, but also for our survival. The day that we stop growing is the day that we begin to die. The truth of the matter is that we have the ability to better ourselves. No matter what area of life we are in, we can make improvements to what we have already done or what has been done to us. There is a quote by St. Jerome that sums this up perfectly, "Good, better, best, never let it rest. Til your good is better, and your better is best."

The value of improving yourself is profoundly displayed in the Rocky Balboa movies, starring Sylvester Stallone. In the films, Rocky was an amateur fighter who had great potential, but he needed something or someone to help him elevate. That elevation did not happen until he met Apollo Creed. Creed was faster, quicker, and an all-around superior fighter. He was one of the best fighters in the world. When Rocky first began training with Creed, Rocky looked like he did not belong. He lost every race, every sparring match, and it seemed like he would not be able to compete with the greats in the boxing world.

However, Rocky was committed and determined to be a world-class boxer. To accomplish his goal, he immersed himself in the world and routines of a world-class boxer, Creed. After continually getting knocked down, Rocky kept getting back up. After each race that he lost, he continued racing Creed, and eventually, after countless hours of diligent work, Rocky was able to defeat Creed. Rocky's experience is a real testament of what a commitment to improving can accomplish.

My mission to get better has put me on a constant journey of personal development, and it has greatly revolutionized my life. By changing distinct negative habits and replacing them with positive ones, I have already shifted my life's trajectory. First, I had to be aware of the fact that I must grow. What if I stayed stuck in my poisonous mind frame? I would have never stepped onto a path of improvement.

Many people have all the talents to become world-class in their field, but they do not make it a mission to reach their highest potential. Oftentimes, people think that they know everything that they need to be successful. They don't have the desire to learn more information, because they have convinced themselves that they already know everything.

"Don't be a know-it-all; be a learn-it-all."
— JUSTIN BARISO

Before we can embark upon the mission of taking it to the next level, we must first acknowledge that there are many levels for us to go to, including to not become a know-it-all. Know-it-alls cannot improve themselves because they feel as if they have reached their supreme level.

As a result, they remain stagnant because of their arrogance. We all know a "know-it-all" or even a few of them. Don't let their type of thinking become your thinking as well. Avoid them and do not let them bring you down with aggravation. Do not attempt to teach "know-it-alls," as they will negate everything you say. Unfortunately, there is no hope for an educated discussion with them. They do not care what research you have, or what book you got your information from; they are right, ALWAYS.

I used to be a know-it-all, and the quality of my life suffered tremendously. I engaged in debates on topics that I knew little about and dared to talk to intellectuals about subjects that they spent years studying. As a result, people began to avoid me because of my arrogance. Do yourself, as well as your future, a favor by not becoming a know-it-all. Equally important, stay away from them.

READ SOMETHING POSITIVE AND INFORMATIONAL DAILY

After we have acknowledged and accepted that we should be on a constant journey to enhance our quality of life, we can now open ourselves to one of the oldest and most effective ways of obtaining knowledge: reading. One of the best things that we can do to improve ourselves is to read positive, informational literature regularly. Ironically, even though people are aware of how essential reading is to self-improvement, the average American only reads about one book a year. However, the top CEOs read more than 60 books a year.

The benefits of reading books are impressive. We get to pick the brains of successful people through the pages that they write. Successful people tell their stories in books. In these books, they lay the blueprint for success, so we can pick up the steps that it takes to reach our desired destination. The irony is that some people want to achieve goals, but do not read the books on how to get there. Instead, they attempt to figure it out on their own rather than learn from someone who has already accomplished their particular goals. I am a big believer in the quote, "It is ok to be a copycat, just as long as we copy the right cat."

There was a point in time when I hated reading. It required too much focus, and I thought that everything that I read was common sense (because I was a know-it-all). Then I realized that reading books is to the brain what lifting weights is to the body. Books make our minds stronger as if it is a muscle. If you do not want to read books, then listen to podcasts or audiobooks. Do not stay weak minded.

ATTEND YOUTUBE UNIVERSITY

Reading books is a vital method of growing and developing mentally. However, various learning methods are more attractive to millennials and those who need alternative techniques for acquiring information. Lucky for us, there is YouTube University (YouTube). Attending YouTube University is free and it can give you a wealth of knowledge. It has been a saving grace for me. I've found my favorite motivational speakers, learned how to strengthen my networking skills, and YouTube has even taught me how to fix my car, which saved me thousands of dollars.

YouTube enables one to learn on the go. You can learn a new language by listening to lessons in your car. You can study by "YouTubing" the subject matter and listening to the concepts. If you are hungry and want to learn, then there is no excuse for not mastering a subject of your liking. If you choose not to do so, then it is because of your lack of focus, which only enhances your laziness.

ATTEND TRAINING SESSIONS AND WORKSHOPS

Reading books and attending "YouTube University" is excellent for our advancement, but my favorite way of obtaining information is by attending live training sessions with the people whom we admire most. The in-person educational experience allows us to get information straight from the horse's mouth, and I prefer to learn from the source. These sessions enable us to witness first-hand the passion and the energy that is in the room. Most importantly, we can ask personalized questions and receive the specific answers that we desire.

Attending seminars and workshops makes you more marketable. Usually, you get a certificate for attending these sessions. You can then add your newfound skill to your resume. People who attend training sessions for growth and development are preparing themselves for advancement. They know that attending seminars and workshops allow them access into an exclusive circle of success-minded people. These success-minded people will make you sharper through association.

MOVE OUT OF YOUR COMFORT ZONE

What use is acquiring knowledge if we don't apply it to help us grow? The application of this newly acquired information is the reason that we seek it anyway. The only way to gauge the effectiveness of our knowledge is to step outside of our comfort zone and apply the information we've learned. Although this may be difficult, mostly because stepping outside of our comfort zone requires being uncomfortable, it is imperative if you are working toward taking your life to the next level. Your comfort zone is your safe space, stepping outside of this zone means the possibility of being stressed out, even minutely. It can be frightening to go into the unknown and face our fears. The thought can be overwhelming, but with the right tools and steps, you will be soaring past your comfort zone in no time.

Stepping outside of our comfort zone is the only way for us to excel and step into our greatness. Best-selling author and speaker, Margie Warrell, teaches us, "In an increasingly competitive, cautious and accelerated world, those who are willing to take risks, step out of their comfort zone and into the discomfort of uncertainty will be those who will reap the biggest rewards."

Once you leave your comfort zone, you will gain insight and acquire immense growth. So why don't most people take the leap of faith and step outside of what makes them comfortable? The truth is, the complacency of comfort feels good. Have you ever laid in bed knowing that you should get up and get the day started, but you stay there anyway? Similarly, it is difficult for us to be uncomfortable, mainly because discomfort feels wrong.

Those who step outside of their comfort zone only experience the feeling of uncertainty temporarily. Most times, we quickly adjust and surprise ourselves by rising to the occasion. Taking calculated risks often gives us a much-needed confidence boost. When we face our FEARs, which is also an acronym that stands for False Evidence Appearing Real, we discover that we are capable of far more than we thought was possible. Our fears are lessons, and we have to learn that there is nothing to fear in the first place but fear itself.

Like most first-time college goers, going to a big school is frightening. I actually cried when my dad initially dropped me off on the campus of Florida Agricultural and Mechanical University. I was so afraid to leave my room, but I'm glad that I eventually stepped outside of my dorm room and found poetry open mics. These experiences led me to being comfortable in speaking amongst large crowds; the more I speak, the better I am.

So many opportunities have been made available to me all because I stepped outside of my comfort zone and decided to try something new. Since then, I have had the confidence to try other things that have gotten me closer to success as a speaker. I have tried comedy, and now my speeches are quite funny. I have attempted to host, and now I am often hired to host events. Stepping outside of your comfort zone will undoubtedly create more opportunities for you.

GET A CAREER COACH/MENTOR

The greatest men and women who have influenced the world have had coaches and mentors to push them to enhance their skill-sets. Tiger Woods has a coach, Michael Jordan has a coach, even the Ball boys have their father, Lavar Ball, coaching them on how to master the game of basketball. When we are in the picture, it is challenging to see the improvements that we need to make. However, a coach notices the smallest details that can help us make the corrections that we overlook.

I am an advocator for apprenticeships, as well as bridging the gap between the young and the old. An apprenticeship is the act of someone who is skilled in an area teaching someone how to be proficient in the same area. Older people are seasoned. I call them seasoned because older people have knowledge that can only be acquired with age. When you have seasoned people in your life, it is beneficial to take advantage of their insight. Find seasoned people and make them a part of your fountain of knowledge. It is extremely beneficial if they are in the position to coach you. Older people have lived longer and offer wisdom that will save you time in achieving your goals.

As a student of life, I find pleasure in seeking seasoned people who find joy in passing the torch to the younger generation. I show them that I am hungry and willing to serve so that they can entrust me with their torch of excellence. My dad, affectionately known as Coach, serves as my pusher. I come to him for advice on life and sometimes for a different viewpoint to challenge my thinking.

"While we teach, we learn."
— SENECA

TEACH

The most effective approach to learning a concept is to teach it to other people. There is a certain depth of knowledge that is required to show someone a new way of learning. Students can learn, but to take on the role of a teacher, you must explain complex ideas in a way that all of the students can grasp. Eventually, you will learn how to teach to different learning styles and diverse personalities. When you master a concept, you can relay the information to almost anyone.

Teaching does more than make you more knowledgeable; it makes you more credible. It opens up substantial opportunities for you to demonstrate your expertise. Before I became a teacher, I learned how to solve a Rubik's Cube. To develop a deeper understanding of the Rubik's Cube and to demonstrate it to others, I began teaching people how to solve it for themselves.

That eventually led me to writing a speech outlining personal development through solving a Rubik's Cube. The outline has since transitioned as a part of my business brand, the completion of this book. Due to my learning how to solve a Rubik's Cube, I have maximized my elasticity for success. It is unbelievable what learning through teaching can turn into and the many doors that can open up because of it.

WHY DO WE NEED TO TAKE IT TO THE NEXT LEVEL?

When we decide to take it to the next level, we make a conscious effort to develop into a higher version of ourselves. We can choose not to reach our acme of success, but the day that we stop growing is the day that we die. A quote that describes this concept states, "Many people die at 25, but they are not buried until they are 65." These people have stopped growing and bettering themselves; hence, they live a life of mediocrity.

They take their skills, talents, and dreams to the graveyard with them to never be developed. Les Brown famously professes, "The graveyard is the richest place on earth, because it is here that you will find all the hopes and dreams that were never fulfilled, the books that were never written, the songs that were never sung, the inventions that were never shared, the cures that were never discovered, all because someone was too afraid to take that first step, keep with the problem, or undetermined to carry out their dream."

INSIDE THE CUBE

1. How do you best learn?
_____
_____

2. What are the skills you need to accomplish your goals?
_____
_____

3. Who has knowledge of those skills?
_____
_____

4. How can you acquire these desired skills?
_____
_____

5. What are your morning and evening routines?
_____
_____

SEE THE BIGGER PICTURES

THE FIRST FOUR STEPS OF solving the Rubik's Cube established a strong foundation and a path to success. People who believe in themselves, have a strong why, surround themselves with positive people who push and motivate them to be better versions of themselves, listen to motivational messages on a daily basis and continue to grow and develop on a consistent basis are on the cusp of greatness. These are foundational principles of many of the successful people in the world.

The fifth step of solving the Rubik's Cube is to see the bigger picture. Seeing the bigger picture means that you keep your commitment to your commitments and finish what you start, in particularly to endure the trials and tribulations of life. When life begins to throw the obstacles and setbacks your way, these are not dead ends. Instead, these are tests for you to develop a testimony and share with others who want to follow in your path. It is those who are resilient that achieve their dreams.

When we plan our journey, we set it as a straight shot to our destination; however, it is never that easy. Life is a series of twists and turns that we sometimes cannot prepare for to the best of our abilities. Surprises, both good and bad, will happen. We rejoice and praise good surprises. We also need to know how to handle the bad surprises.

The most successful people are those who endure the storms of life and relentlessly reach a triumphant victory. Such an experience will create a success-story that encourages others who suffer from similar afflictions to continue to conquer their obstacles. When life gives you a test, turn it into a testimony to encourage others to endure life's trials with a positive outlook. If other people can overcome the lowest of lows, then it is possible for you to do so as well.

One of life's most difficult tasks is to remain committed to your responsibilities, especially during adversity. Life can be tough if we allow it to be. With the challenges of managing money, relationships, careers and a slew of other things, we tend to become overwhelmed by the twists and turns of life. Even if we practice the first four steps of solving the Rubik's Cube, life will persist in introducing new storms to our world.

This step is personal and transparent with a season of storms that I thought would break me. Instead, that season of turmoil strengthened me significantly. I learned to turn my pain into power. I redirected that pain to serve as motivation to elevate to new heights. I was blessed, fortunate, and highly favored enough to have stumbled upon a formula that helped me to solve the Rubik's Cube of life.

I often ponder on reasons why many people, including myself, have quit and thrown in the towel. Some of the reasons included tragedies such as death, divorce, or loss of a job. During these tragic moments, it is vital to develop a plan of action to dig yourself out of emotional turmoil. You cannot afford to allow your turmoil to drive you into a depression where you are not productive in chasing your goals.

When I hit rock bottom, I decided to use that low point as a foundation on which to build. Any professional architect will tell you that the way to constructing an immovable building is by ensuring that the foundation of the land is as durable as possible.

Another reason that people abandon their goals is that they allow distractions to deter them from realizing the big picture. I have made it a mission to study the factors that make successful people successful. Through my research, I have learned that they master their breaking point and stay committed to their goals by avoiding distractions. To uphold our commitment, we must maximize our discipline. When the world around us is falling apart, successful people find a way to not fall apart with it.

Life will throw unexpected adversities that will break you if you let it, and it will cause you to abandon your life's mission. You will question God and ask the million-dollar question, "Why me?" However, the question should not be, "Why me?" but, "What is this teaching me?" Some people do not have the mental prowess to view the real value of prevailing through the storms of life. However, to adequately solve the Rubik's Cube inside, you must remain malleable and resilient. Catastrophic life events are not only designed to expand you personally, but also others who may be affected either immediately or in future generations.

Sometimes we go through storms at, seemingly, the worst time. After I graduated from the Masters of History program at FAMU, I decided to embark on the path of becoming an educator, a career that I hold in high esteem and have always wanted to pursue. I've had a slew of influential educators, for as long as I can remember, who have made all the difference for me versus many of my childhood friends. Consequently, I desired to offer the same dynamic impact on my future students. So, I joined Teach For America to pursue my passion.

I left Tallahassee with tears in my eyes. Atlanta is where I was born and raised, but Tallahassee is where I became a man. Earning my degree was the passport to accessing my lifelong dream of becoming an educator. I began my teaching career in Atlanta, and like most first-time teachers, I was just as nervous as the children. There had to be at least a million questions racing through my mind. How do I manage my class? How do I earn the students' respect? How do I effectively teach 200 students? I studied the works of some of the greatest educators that the world has known: Geoffrey Canada, Marva Collins, and Ron Clark. Their books were like pedagogical bibles for a novice educator. Everyone assured me that teaching would be one of the most difficult, yet impactful experiences of my life. But no one prepared me for the calamity that would ensue in my personal life.

"GOD DOES NOT GIVE HEAVY BURDENS TO WEAK PEOPLE."

Les Brown has professed that, "In life, you're either going through a problem, just left a problem or headed towards one." It was not long before I would personify the essence of the quote. My two years of teaching was one of the most challenging periods of my life. Within a year's time frame, I lost my mother and uncle due to cancer, the man who raised me was diagnosed with stage four cancer and my wife confessed that she no longer wanted to be married to me. I fell into an abyss of depression, and I constantly questioned God and wondered why I was punished so harshly.

It all began after I got a deeply disturbing call from my mother, who was living in Alabama at the time. She called to inform me that she had stage four ovarian cancer. Since my mother could not receive treatment in Alabama, she moved to Georgia with my wife and me, where treatment was available for her. She began treatment a few days after moving in, causing her body to begin to decline immediately. I saw her get weaker by the day.

Then, one day at work, my neighbor called and told me that my mother had died. My wife walked into her room, and she was lying on the floor, her body was stiff and cold. It hurts to lose your mother at such a young age. I wanted my children to develop a relationship with their grandmother because I longed for one with mine. Unfortunately, I never got the chance to meet my grandmother because she passed away before I was born.

My mother made Sunday dinners that would make your stomach smile, and I would give anything to have a home cooked meal from her. Honor, love, and cherish your parents because you never know when it will be their time to transition from this planet.

I felt like I was compelled to do so much more as a son while my mother was still alive. As a child, I witnessed my mother work hard, and she never complained about raising three boys by herself. I wanted to expose her to an entire world outside of Atlanta. Sometimes I think that it is unfair to have lost my mother to cancer when I was just 25 years old. I wanted my children to know what it's like to have a wonderful grandmother, to experience her loving ways, and her delicious Sunday dinners. My mother is always with me in spirit, and I will honor her by adopting her work ethic.

Shortly before my mother's death, I received another heart-dropping phone call. My dad, Coach Hill, had been hospitalized after passing out at work. Then I found out my dad had developed stage four cancer of the liver. I was terrified. I had just lost my mother, and now the man who raised me as his own was also in a life-threatening situation. I questioned

God and wondered, "Why Me? Why did I have to experience so much pain and agony?"

Coach Hill was not my biological father, but he raised me as such. There is a difference between a father and a dad. A father will help in creating you, but a dad raises you. Coach Hill has a family of his own, but he raised me. I probably would not be where I am if it had not been for everything he invested in me.

One of the most challenging times of our lives is when the weight of the world is already on our shoulder, and God feels the need to add more weight. That is exactly what he did in my life. He added more weight to me. There were so many tragedies thrown at me at one time that I began to feel numb to the pain. Even worse, I normalized the numbness, especially as the trials kept coming in one by one.

Not long after I processed the news and tragic loss of those I loved dearly, I received a phone call from my cousin that my uncle was in the hospital. His health had deteriorated and was preparing to transition after his diagnosis of cancer. He was my mother's only brother. I had so much pain and grief in my heart that I just couldn't attend another funeral.

When the school year ended, I treated that time as a period of healing. I wanted to grieve properly and prepare myself for the next school year. I wanted my students to see someone who overcomes tragedy and can still be a productive member of society. I saw my students making excuses about why they could not perform at their peak, and justifying their lackluster performance. I wanted to be their example of triumphing through the tragedy.

As soon as I thought that the tragedy would be over, God decided to place more burdens on my life. The next disaster almost broke me entirely. The birth of a child, coupled with the agony of death of several family members, is difficult to bear. My marriage began to suffer, and we just could not be there for each other emotionally the way we needed to be. As a result, my wife, the mother of my children, decided that she could no longer be married to me and that we needed to divorce. Dealing with a divorce is heart wrenching. It almost feels like you have lost a limb when you lose your spouse. Having two young children does not make it any easier. I had to deal with the fact that my family was no longer with me.

Now, my ex-wife and I are friendly towards each other. The pain of divorce has settled in, and we are learning to be cordial co-parents to our two beautiful children. At first, I didn't think that I would make it. I was still grieving the loss of my uncle and mother. My dad was suffering from cancer, and I could lose him sooner than expected. I was sad and depressed all of the time. My students suffered, even though I tried to keep it together for them.

Then something happened that changed my perspective on life and my situation. I heard a quote while listening to motivational speeches. "God does not give heavy burdens to weak people." That reinforced my belief that God had something more significant planned for me. I realized that I was supposed to use the tests that I endured and turn them into a testimony. People needed to hear this story of my triumph through my tragedy so that they too can be encouraged to battle life and come out strong after the fight. So, I decided to take the advice that I offer people and compose this book.

This book was written during some of the darkest moments of my life. It was therapeutic for me to share my stories and know that someone else could benefit from my experiences. Sometimes when I was writing, my pages would be stained with tears. I often tell people, writing for me has been a gift and a curse. Although these are accomplishments, I sometimes wonder if the pain that inspires these stories is worth it. Then, I pray and receive the revelation that God has used me as a vessel to tell a story that would encourage others to chase their greatness. Albeit there will be tragedies chasing you, never cease to go after your dreams. It will get hard, but there is light at the end of the tunnel.

To take it a step further, and make the pages of this book a reality, I enrolled in a doctoral program at FAMU in pursuance of a PhD in Educational Leadership. It is truly a blessing and an honor to be in a doctoral program at a school that I thought I had no business at. Turns out, attending FAMU was the greatest decision that I could have made. I am grateful for the many blessings that have been bestowed on me as a result of not quitting.

My faith is strong. My painful tragedies have made me powerful and triumphant. The current goal that I am focused on is graduating from this doctoral program. I am still learning how to solve the twists and turns of life. We may sometimes fluctuate between the steps of solving the Rubik's Cube, especially as we get closer to meeting our goals, living our dreams and obtaining our aspirations. The key is to stay true to the process and keep your commitment to your commitments. You can't live the life that you believe you deserve if you quit.

Too many people give up right before they have reached their destiny. The people in life who win are those who do not quit. There is no doubt that it'll get hard, but if you keep pushing and striving, then you will achieve one of the hardest puzzles in the world.

At that moment, you will be rewarded for your hard work and will have solved the Rubik's Cube inside of you.

INSIDE THE CUBE

1. What are tragedies in your life that you had to endure?

   _____

   _____

2. Identify moments in your life where you felt like a failure.

   _____

   _____

3. What are your biggest distractions?

   _____

   _____

4. What kind of environment do you need to be completely focused?

   _____

   _____

5. How can you keep your commitment to your commitment?

   _____

   _____

DO NOT TAKE THE STICKERS OFF

SINCE THE RUBIK'S CUBE INCEPTION, there have been a slew of people who have attempted to solve it, but only a few have accomplished the feat. Some people battled through the mental frustrations of the Rubik's Cube's twist and turns and eventually learned how to solve the Cube. Then there are others who have opted to solve the Rubik's Cube differently, by removing the stickers. Taking off the stickers only results in a ruined Rubik's Cube. Trying to solve life's Rubik's Cube by taking off the stickers only results in a ruined life. In other words, you can't cheat your way to success.

Motivational speaker and salesman, Joe Girard, states, "The elevator to success is out of order. You'll have to use the stairs ... one step at a time." Anything worth having in life is worth working hard for and making sacrifices to get. The reward for enduring trials and tribulations is gratifying. On the contrary, taking shortcuts in life are deemed to lead to dead-end roads. I'm sure that you know someone who possesses an innate genius level that endows them with tremendous talents. However, they find pleasure in taking shortcuts in lieu of grinding and pushing through the obstacles for what it is that they desire. This is why Albert Einstein once said, "Genius is 1 percent talent and 99 percent effort."

There is no substitute for hard work. If you wish to be great at something, you have to work at what you want to be great at. Legendary basketball player, Larry Bird, would go to the gym every morning and shoot 500 free throws before his first class. Venus and Serena Williams would routinely wake up at 6:00 a.m. in order to practice tennis before school and would continue practicing again after school. They started this routine when they were just eight years old. Despite having enough money to do whatever he wants to do, Elon Musk works between 80 and 100 hours a week operating Tesla and SpaceX. Hard work is a determining factor in whether or not someone will become successful.

"DON'T CHASE THE BIG BREAK, CHASE THE DAILY DISCIPLINE."

Adrien Brody once said, "It takes fifteen years to become an overnight success." Sometimes we view successful people as getting a lucky break or they were simply given an opportunity without earning it first. This is rarely the case. Most successful people put in years of long nights and no social life in order to make their dreams become a reality.

People who chase shortcuts are often duped into believing that if they can catch that one big break, then they will accelerate to success effortlessly. Many people chase their big break by playing the lottery and others participate in get-rich-quick schemes. None of these shortcuts lay a foundation that is duplicable for others to emulate and obtain success. The adage that best sums up this case states, "Don't chase the big break, chase the daily discipline." Instead of looking for shortcuts to success, follow the five steps outlined in this book; they are foolproof.

If you are looking for an easy way to accomplish your goals, then you are essentially giving up. When you are chasing success, it is guaranteed that you will be uncomfortable. Thus, if you are aspiring to be successful, find comfort in being uncomfortable. There is something about battling the storms of life that allows you to appreciate the journey that much more. The profound philosopher, J. Cole, teaches us that, "There is beauty in the struggle."

Once you realize that there are no easy routes to success, you will learn to appreciate the hard times. These moments will challenge you and they will change you. The big tasks often prepare you for big success. Each struggle that you experience is there to teach you a lesson. Learn from the lesson and use it to make yourself better. These life lessons can be compared to a bow and arrow. An arrow can only be shot when it is pulled backwards. When you let the arrow go, it is launched forward with a penetrating force. Sometimes life will pull us backwards with trials and tribulations, but eventually it will launch you forward if you will stay focused and stay aimed at your goals.

Sometimes people allow themselves to be content with their life and they settle for the way things are. Even though they are fully aware that there could be a greater life awaiting them, they instead choose to allow their decision to settle for mediocrity to prevent them from accomplishing their inner desires.

Les Brown once said, "The graveyard is the richest place on earth, because it is here that you will find all the hopes and dreams that were never fulfilled, the books that were never written, the songs that were never sung, the inventions that were never shared, the cures that were never discovered, all because someone was too afraid to take that first step, keep with the problem, or determined to carry out their dream."

When I die, I want to die on empty. What I mean by this is that I want to have accomplished everything on my list. The biggest regret on most people's deathbeds is that they never attempted to chase their dreams because they were too content with being mediocre and settled for less than they were capable of. Anything worth having is worth working for. And, yes, it will be hard. However, the hard things that we do, most often provide the greatest benefit to our lives. You owe it to yourself, to your family, and most importantly to God, do not take the easy way out; rather, strive for even more than you thought you were capable of.

In addition to settling for mediocrity, we can also sometimes fall victim to leaving everything to chance and failing to plan. There is an old but useful proverb that says, "When we fail to plan, we plan to fail." Life is not the luck of the draw or a gamble. Sometimes there are outliers who get a lucky break, but in most cases, their lives are not improved because they have not learned how to establish the principles that will make and keep you successful.

Do not let fate or destiny decide your life. You are responsible for you destiny, and you control your own fate. Just because you wish for something to happen does not mean that you will automatically get what you want in the future. The late preacher and motivational speaker, Myles Monroe, once said, "We do not plan our future, instead we plan our habits and our habits determine our future." If you plan to have a bright future, then you must prepare for it in the present.

Cherish the moments of trying and failing; you will fail your way to success. By permitting yourself to fail, you are allowing yourself to try new things, and as you try new things, you learn new things.

As an educator, I witness a system that teaches our students that failing is wrong. Such a concept stifles a person's creativity, imagination, and their ability or desire to try new things. We have taught our students to fear failure, and as a result, they resort to an easy route to avoid it. However, as a student of life, you must understand that a bank of failures is the passageway to an abundance of success. As a matter of fact, failure and success are in the same direction. Thomas Edison stated, "I did not fail a thousand times, I simply found a thousand ways that did not work."

While failing can lead to your success, it can also be overwhelming. It takes a truly committed person with a "don't quit" attitude to go from failure to failure to failure without losing hope, passion, and persistence. Face failure with confidence, and learn from your mistakes as you fail.

FAILURE IS THE PREREQUISITE TO SUCCESS

There is a reason why the letter F comes before the letter S in the alphabet; you will never reach success without failing an exponential number of times. However, when you position your failures to align with your pathway to success, then the stench of failure is no longer present.

A clear example is one of America's favorite beverages, Coca-Cola. The creator of Coca-Cola, John Pemberton, initially created the soft drink for pharmaceutical purposes. Pemberton met little pharmaceutical success; nearly every one of his drugs plunged into the sea of failure before consumers learned of their existence. Since he was not able to capitalize off of the standard practices of medicine, he shifted his direction to meet a need that Americans were demanding: a vibrant alternative to liquor while in bars. Unfortunately, Pemberton was deficient in advertising and died before his product would become the household name that it is now.

However, Asa Griggs Candler, an acute advertiser, assumed ownership of the entire Coca-Cola brand and transcended its presence in the marketplace. If it were not for Pemberton's unwavering belief in the value of Coca-Cola despite its many failures, Candler would not have taken on the company. He registered the formula to be sold solely as a non-medicinal beverage, which compelled consumers to associate it with leisure activities. Sales began to skyrocket, the brand became an international sensation, and Coca-Cola products are probably the most popular beverages in the world. Pemberton's failure helped establish a massive legacy for his product.

It took over a decade for Coca-Cola to become one of the premier companies in business. However, the company became successful because its pioneers remained consistent and never quit even when it seemed like the company would not prosper.

Failing will let you know how bad you want to succeed. Can you go from failure to failure and keep the same persistence and determination without quitting? Or is failure enough for you to throw in the towel and quit? Sometimes people think that they are willing to work hard in order to achieve their goals until they fail for the first time. When they fail, they feel that chasing their goals, dreams, and aspirations are not as important as they once thought before. However, those that endure failure and use it as motivation to push them towards success are those who muster together the ingredients to reach success.

Those who are able to use failure as inspiration understand that failure can make you stronger. Most people let the trials and tribulations of failure convince them to avoid ever trying anything again. Those who overcome their failures witness a firsthand account of their own strength. Once you experience a growth in confidence from accomplishing something that you previously failed at, you now have the belief that you can accomplish new things that test your strength.

After dropping out of FAMU and flunking out of GSU, I realized that I had failed and did not think that I would be able to dig myself out of the hole that I had dug for myself. After realizing how poorly I had done academically, I decided that I had an obligation to myself, and to the people who believed in me, to do better because I knew that I could do better. After failing, I realized that I did not want the future that lay before me if I did not take my education seriously. This was my wakeup call. There were so many doors that had closed on me and all that I had wanted to do, simply because I quit after failing. The only true failing is quitting after failing.

I almost quit on myself too when I failed. However, Les Browns words, "Just because you fail, it does not mean that you are a failure," motivated me and gave me the strength to turn my test into a testimony. Now I am currently in pursuit of my PhD all because I had the resiliency to bounce back from my failures and learn from my mistakes.

While there is no such thing as perfection, failing can always enhance us to make progress in our lives. As an avid chess player, the game teaches me a lot of life skills. One of my mentors has a chess quote that is also applicable to life. "In chess you either win or you learn." The same principle can be applied to life, if applied correctly. In life you either win or you learn. This is because your mistakes allow you to analyze your weaknesses and work on them. This allows you to see where you went wrong and how you can make improvements on yourself.

Lastly, failure allows us to realize that failing is not the end of the world. As a matter of fact, the sooner you fail, the sooner you realize that you can bounce back from your failures. Failing can make you seem helpless and hopeless, but after experiencing failing a few times, you would soon come to realize that failure is a part of living and that we need failure in order to succeed.

"Every human life is made to fit someplace, and there is a place for every life."
— ASA GRIGGS CANDLER

INSIDE THE CUBE

1. What are some shortcuts that you could take to your goals?
_____
_____

2. What are the consequences of taking shortcuts to your goals?
_____
_____

3. Where can you post your goals and see them every day?
_____
_____

4. How can you find extra time in your day for accomplishing your goals?
_____
_____

5. What is your personal consequence for quitting on your goals?
_____
_____

SOLVING THE RUBIK'S CUBE, STILL to this day, is one of the most impressive acts to accomplish. However, this is not about simply solving the Rubik's Cube. Instead, it is about solving problems or challenges in your life and accomplishing feats that you once thought were impossible.

I have had the honor, privilege, and pleasure to teach over 300 students how to solve the Rubik's Cube, and in each case, something magical happened that will hopefully alter their trajectory for the better. Most of these students did not think that they could do it. Many of them ruled themselves out before even getting started.

However, one by one, students started learning how to solve the Rubik's Cube, and other students started to take notice. Eventually more and more students began to believe that they could solve it, and they did. It was beautiful to see students walking down the hallways with Rubik's Cubes in their hands, solving them with ease. All of these students experienced a spike in their confidence levels. They were so proud to showcase their new skills to their parents and their teachers.

One day I charged my students to apply the Rubik's Cube to their lives. They learned how to solve the Rubik's Cube, a task that they swore was impossible. I then challenged them to apply that same level of commitment and determination that they used in solving the Rubik's Cube to solving their schoolwork, and they did. Many of the students began to do better academically, and their confidence levels rose, that made the difference. These students now believed in themselves, and that belief elevated them to be not just better students, but better people.

The principles in *Life is Like A Rubik's Cube* have elevated the quality of my life for the better. Before implementing these concepts, I was a dropout at one school and a flunk out at another. I had no clear vision, no dreams to motivate me, and no clear trajectory to my future, and now I have all three. My vision is clearer than ever, my dreams wake me up and give me a relentless drive, and I am proud of my trajectory.

One of the lessons that I am learning while in my PhD program is that real leaders develop other people into leaders. I pray that you too can digest the steps outlined in this book, personalize them, and use them for your advancement in life. Too many people are sitting on the sidelines because they have not yet learned how to "solve the Rubik's Cube inside of them." The twists and turns of life sometimes scare people to not take action, but these twists and turns are oftentimes easier than we thought. We just need to believe in ourselves and take action.

Reading this book is important, and will definitely improve the quality of your life if used properly. To fully take advantage of *Life is Like A Rubik's Cube*, take the time to answer the questions at the end of each step. These questions will help you develop a true sense of self, and in order to know what it is you are meant to do, you must first know who you are. Thank you for taking the time to invest in yourself by investing in this book. Be safe like a bank vault, hold it down like short people doing pushups, and PEACE!

Recap:

1. **Belief**: Have an undying belief in yourself. Know that you can accomplish your goals and dreams and aspirations, and walk, act and think like you are deserving of them.

2. **Solve Your Cross**: Establish the reasons why you will accomplish your goals. Identify the people that you want to make proud, the people that you want to prove wrong, and every reason why you must accomplish your goals, dreams, and aspirations. When you feel the urge to quit, think about the reasons why you must not, and use them as motivation to keep going.

3. **Fill in Your Corners**: Immerse yourself in a positive environment. Surround yourself with quality people who want to see you win. Remove negative, toxic people from your life. In addition, listen to motivational messages on a daily basis. You are what you are and where you are because of what you allow to go into your mind, and if you want to change what you are and where you are, then you must change what you allow to go into your mind.

4. **Take It to the Next Level**: Continue to grow and get better. Never be content with where you are in life. Make it a mission to always obtain more knowledge and skills. The day that we stop growing is the day that we begin to die.

5. **See the Bigger Picture**: Stay committed to your commitments. Do not become distracted by the storms of life. Do not let the trials and tribulations of life prevent you from accomplishing your goals, dreams and aspirations. In

the words of the great motivational speaker Les Brown, "It's not over until I win!"

6. **Don't Take Off the Stickers**: There are no shortcuts in life. Shortcuts lead to dead ends. Follow the steps of solving the Rubik's Cube, and you will soon be able to solve the Rubik's Cubes inside of you.

Made in the USA
Columbia, SC
04 November 2024

45407194R00057